Theory Paper Grade 4   1996   A

Duration 2 hours

Candidates should answer ALL questions.
Write your answers on this paper — no others will be accepted.
Answers must be written clearly and neatly — otherwise marks may be lost.

TOTAL MARKS
100

1 (a) Rewrite the following from bar 2, grouping the notes correctly.

10

Haydn, *The Creation*

(b) Rewrite the following in notes and rests of *twice the value*, and complete the new time signature.

2 **EITHER**

(a) Write a rhythm on one note, with time signature and bar-lines, to fit these words.
Write each syllable under the note or notes to which it is to be sung.

10

And ever she sung from noon to noon,
'Two red roses across the moon'.   *Morris*

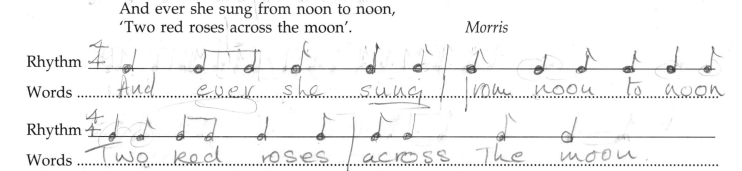

Rhythm

Words ......And......ever......she......sung......from......noon......to......noon

Rhythm

Words ......Two......red......roses......across......the......moon.

OR

(b) Write a four-bar rhythm in ⅞ time. Include the following groups of notes in your rhythm:

3 Name each of the following notes, as in the given example.

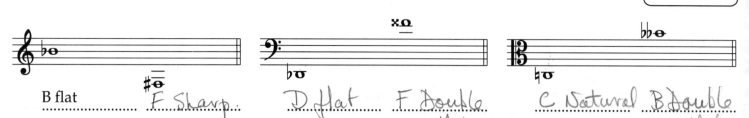

B flat   F Sharp   D. flat   F. Double   C. Natural   B. Double
                                              Hat   Hat

4 Rewrite the following using the alto clef but keeping the pitch the same.

Shostakovich, Symphony No. 5

© Boosey & Hawkes Music Publishers Ltd
reprinted by permission

5 Write the scales named below, using the given rhythm.

B major, ascending, without key signature but adding any necessary sharp or flat signs

F minor melodic, ascending, with key signature

6 (a) Write as minims (half notes) the notes named from the scale of B♭ minor harmonic, [10]
as in the given example. Do *not* use a key signature.

tonic · · · · · · · · · · · mediant · · · · · · · · · leading note · · · · · · · · · dominant

(b) Describe fully each of the following intervals.

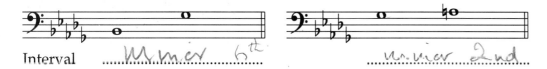

Interval ......Mi.Mor...6ᵗʰ...................Mn.Mior...2nd...

7 (a) Name each of the numbered chords as tonic, subdominant or dominant. [10]
The key is G minor.

W. Ballet, *Lute-book Lullaby*

(1) (2)   (3)

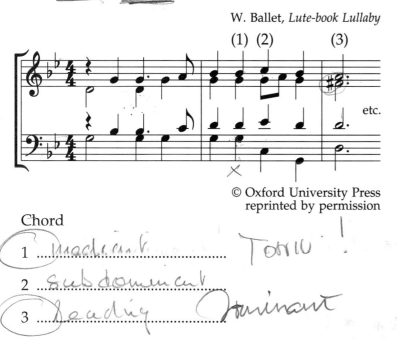

etc.

© Oxford University Press
reprinted by permission

Chord

1 ....Medicant.......... Tonic

2 ...Subdominant....

3 ...Leading........... dominant

(b) Write the key signature and the named triad in C♯ minor.

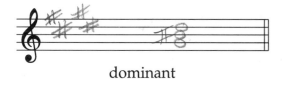

dominant

5

8 The following is an extract from the first movement of Franck's Symphony.
Look at it and then answer the questions below.

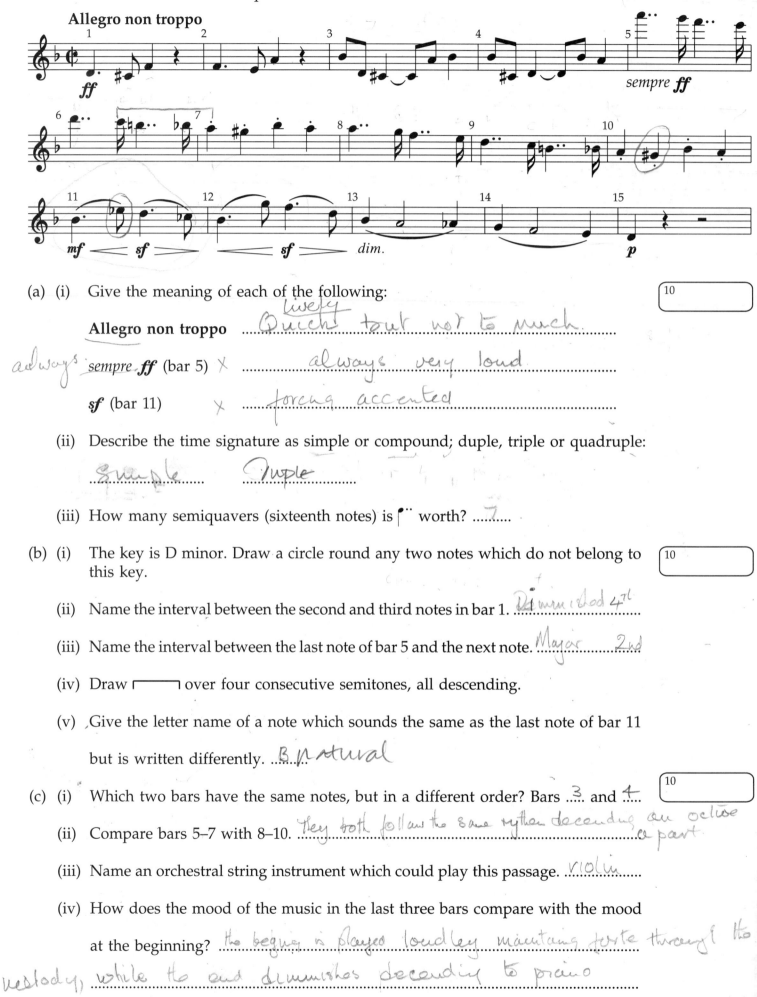

(a) (i) Give the meaning of each of the following:

10

Allegro non troppo ...... *lively* Quick tout not to much.

always **sempre** *ff* (bar 5) ✗ ...... always very loud

sf (bar 11) ✗ ...... forcing accented

(ii) Describe the time signature as simple or compound; duple, triple or quadruple:

...... Simple ...... Triple ......

(iii) How many semiquavers (sixteenth notes) is ♪·· worth? ......7......

(b) (i) The key is D minor. Draw a circle round any two notes which do not belong to this key.

10

(ii) Name the interval between the second and third notes in bar 1. ...... Diminished 4th

(iii) Name the interval between the last note of bar 5 and the next note. ...... Major 2nd

(iv) Draw ⌐‾‾¬ over four consecutive semitones, all descending.

(v) Give the letter name of a note which sounds the same as the last note of bar 11

but is written differently. ...... B. Natural

(c) (i) Which two bars have the same notes, but in a different order? Bars ...3... and ...4...

10

(ii) Compare bars 5–7 with 8–10. ...... They both follow the same rythm decending an octive ...... a part

(iii) Name an orchestral string instrument which could play this passage. ...... Violin

(iv) How does the mood of the music in the last three bars compare with the mood

at the beginning? ...... the begning is played loudley mantaing forte through the

melody, while the end diminishes decending to piano

6

Theory Paper Grade 4   1996   B

Duration 2 hours

Candidates should answer ALL questions.
Write your answers on this paper — no others will be accepted.
Answers must be written clearly and neatly — otherwise marks may be lost.

TOTAL MARKS
100

1 (a) Add the time signature at the beginning of each of these extracts from Sibelius's [10]
Second Symphony. Both begin on the first beat of the bar.

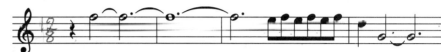

© Breitkopf & Härtel
reprinted by permission

(b) Rewrite the following in notes of *half the value*, and add the new time signature.
Also describe the time (simple or compound; duple, triple or quadruple).

Bartók, Divertimento

© Boosey & Hawkes Music Publishers Ltd
reprinted by permission

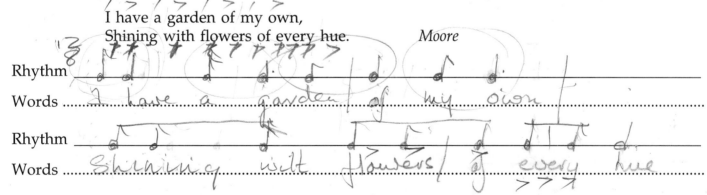

Time ......Compoud triple......

2 **EITHER**
(a) Write a rhythm on one note, with time signature and bar-lines, to fit these words. [10]
Write each syllable under the note or notes to which it is to be sung.

I have a garden of my own,
Shining with flowers of every hue.   *Moore*

Rhythm _____

Words ......I have a garden of my own......

Rhythm _____

Words ......Shining with flowers of every hue......

OR
(b) Write a four-bar rhythm in $\frac{2}{2}$ time. Include the following note and group of notes in your rhythm:

⌐3⌐
♩.. and ♩♩♩

/ = short
> = long

$\frac{2}{2}$ _____

3 Name each of the following notes, as in the given example.

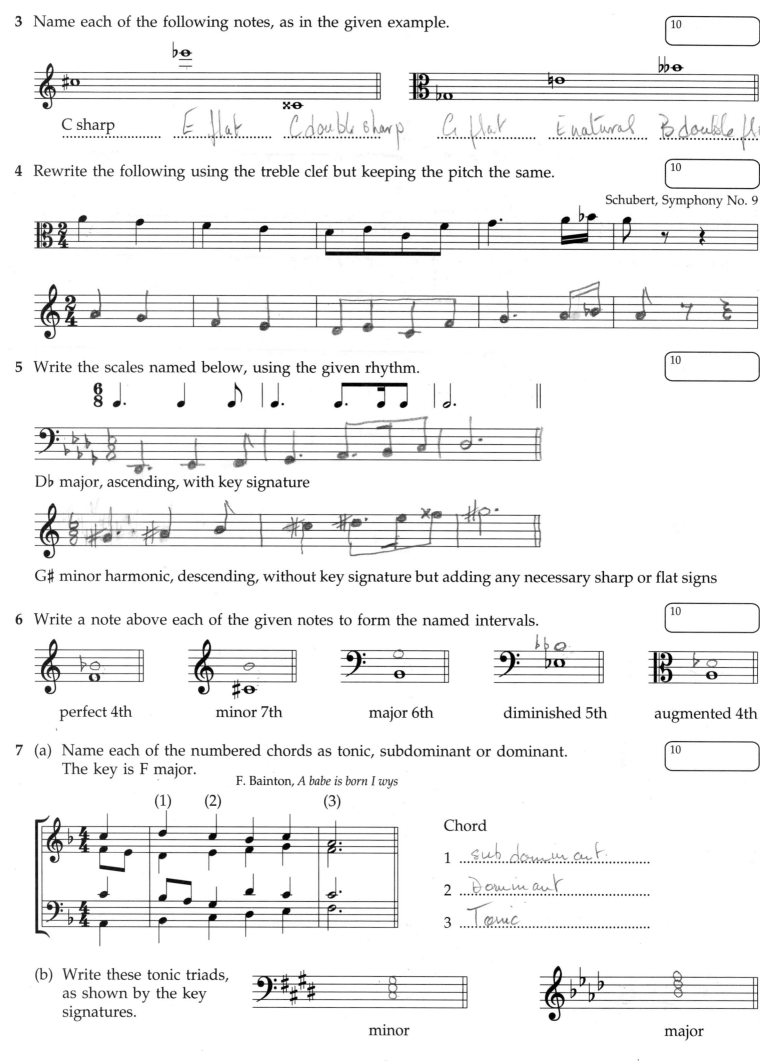

C sharp _____ E flat _____ C double sharp _____ G flat _____ E natural _____ B double flat

4 Rewrite the following using the treble clef but keeping the pitch the same.

10

Schubert, Symphony No. 9

5 Write the scales named below, using the given rhythm.

10

Db major, ascending, with key signature

G# minor harmonic, descending, without key signature but adding any necessary sharp or flat signs

6 Write a note above each of the given notes to form the named intervals.

10

perfect 4th   minor 7th   major 6th   diminished 5th   augmented 4th

7 (a) Name each of the numbered chords as tonic, subdominant or dominant.
The key is F major.

10

F. Bainton, *A babe is born I wys*

(1) (2)   (3)

Chord

1 ...sub dominant...

2 ...Dominant...

3 ...Tonic...

(b) Write these tonic triads,
as shown by the key
signatures.

minor   major

8

8 Here is the beginning of a melody in the style of a Spanish dance called a Seguidilla. It is sung by Carmen, the leading character in the opera of the same name by Bizet.
Look at it and then answer the questions below.

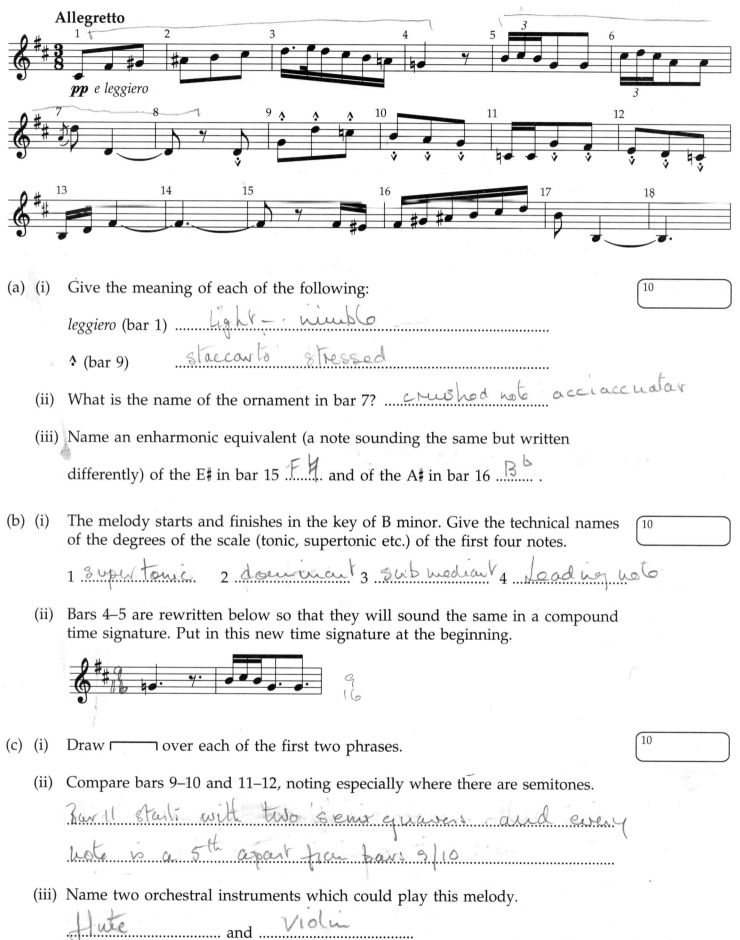

(a) (i)   Give the meaning of each of the following: 10

   leggiero (bar 1) ......Light — nimble...

   ⌃ (bar 9) ......staccato stressed..

   (ii)   What is the name of the ornament in bar 7? ......crushed note acciaccatar

   (iii) Name an enharmonic equivalent (a note sounding the same but written

   differently) of the E♯ in bar 15 ...F♮... and of the A♯ in bar 16 ...B♭... .

(b) (i)   The melody starts and finishes in the key of B minor. Give the technical names   10
   of the degrees of the scale (tonic, supertonic etc.) of the first four notes.

   1 .super tonic.   2 .dominant. 3 .sub mediant. 4 .leading note.

   (ii) Bars 4–5 are rewritten below so that they will sound the same in a compound
   time signature. Put in this new time signature at the beginning.

   9
   16

(c) (i)   Draw ⌐‾‾⌐ over each of the first two phrases.   10

   (ii) Compare bars 9–10 and 11–12, noting especially where there are semitones.

   .Bar 11 starts with two semi quavers and every.
   .note is a 5th apart from bars 9/10.

   (iii) Name two orchestral instruments which could play this melody.

   .Flute.............. and ...Violin.........................

9

Theory Paper Grade 4 1996 C

Duration 2 hours

Candidates should answer ALL questions.
Write your answers on this paper — no others will be accepted.
Answers must be written clearly and neatly — otherwise marks may be lost.

TOTAL MARKS
100

1 (a) Complete the time signature and add the missing bar-line to the following.

10

J. S. Bach, *The Well-Tempered Clavier*, Part II, Prelude No. 21

etc.

(b) Rewrite bars 1 and 2 in notes of *twice the value,* and complete the new time signature.

2 **EITHER**
   (a) Write a rhythm on one note, with time signature and bar-lines, to fit these words.
        Write each syllable under the note or notes to which it is to be sung.

10

The animals went in one by one,
There's one more river to cross.   *Song*

OR
(b) Write a four-bar rhythm in ⁴⁄₈ time. Include the following groups of notes in your rhythm:

3 Name each of the following notes, as in the given example.

10

D flat ...... F double sharp   D flat C natural   D sharp G double flat

10

4 Rewrite the following using the bass clef but keeping the pitch the same.

Britten, Cello Symphony

© Boosey & Hawkes Music Publishers Ltd
reprinted by permission

5 Add the correct clefs and any necessary sharp or flat signs to make the scales named below. Do not use key signatures.

B♭ minor melodic

B major

6 (a) Write a chromatic scale in crotchets (quarter notes), beginning and ending on the given notes. Take notice of the key signature and do not use any unnecessary accidentals.

(b) Describe fully each of the following intervals.

Interval   Augmented 4th   ....   Major 7th   ....

7 (a) Name each of the numbered chords as tonic, subdominant or dominant. The key is F major.

Carol, *A great and mighty wonder*

(1) (2)   (3)

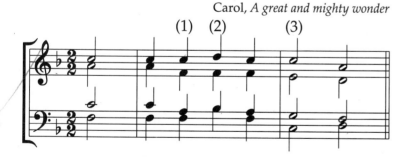

Chord

1 Tonic ....

2 Sub dominant ....

3 dominant ....

(b) Write the named triads without key signatures. Remember to add any necessary sharp or flat signs.

B minor
subdominant triad

F♯ minor
dominant triad

11

8 The following extract is the left-hand melody from Chopin's Prelude in B minor for piano.
Look at it and then answer the questions below.

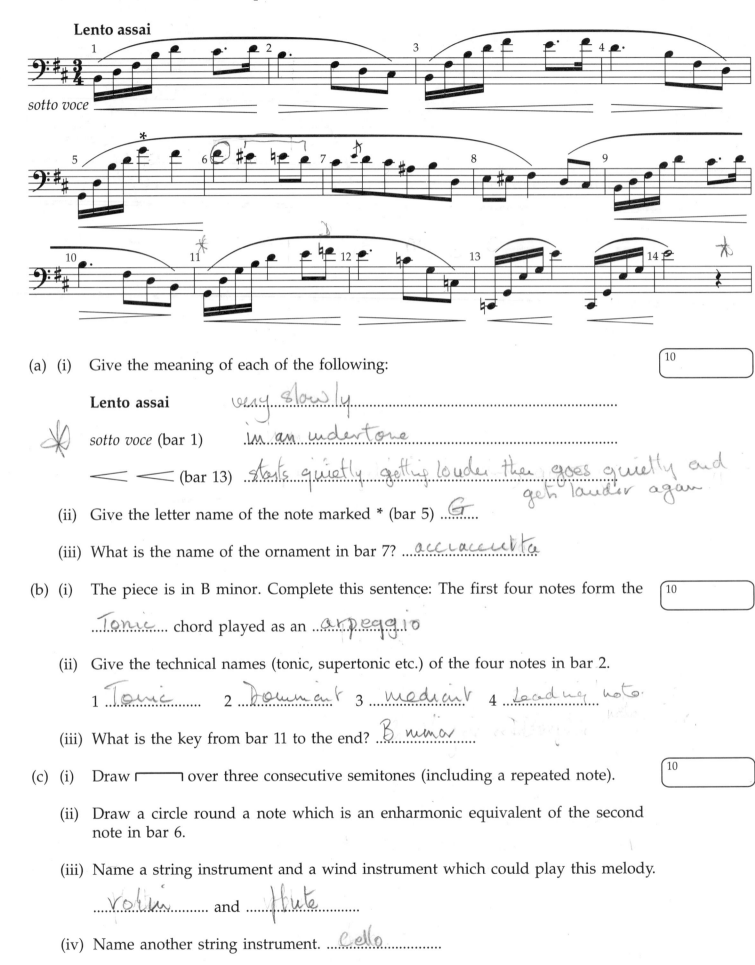

(a) (i) Give the meaning of each of the following:

10

Lentoassai *very slowly*

✳ *sotto voce* (bar 1) *in an undertone*

〈 〈 (bar 13) *starts quietly getting louder then goes quietly and
get louder again*

(ii) Give the letter name of the note marked * (bar 5) ..*G*..

(iii) What is the name of the ornament in bar 7? ..*acciaccatta*..

(b) (i) The piece is in B minor. Complete this sentence: The first four notes form the

10

..*Tonic*.. chord played as an ..*arpeggio*..

(ii) Give the technical names (tonic, supertonic etc.) of the four notes in bar 2.

1 ..*Tonic*.. 2 ..*Dominant*.. 3 ..*mediant*.. 4 ..*Leading note.*..

(iii) What is the key from bar 11 to the end? ..*B minor*..

(c) (i) Draw ⌐‾‾⌐ over three consecutive semitones (including a repeated note).

10

(ii) Draw a circle round a note which is an enharmonic equivalent of the second
note in bar 6.

(iii) Name a string instrument and a wind instrument which could play this melody.

..*violin*.. and ..*flute*..

(iv) Name another string instrument. ..*Cello*..

Theory Paper Grade 4   1996   S

Duration 2 hours

Candidates should answer ALL questions.
Write your answers on this paper — no others will be accepted.
Answers must be written clearly and neatly — otherwise marks may be lost.

1 Each of the following examples starts on the first beat of the bar.

10

   (a) Add the missing bar-lines.

Shostakovich, Symphony No. 5

© Boosey & Hawkes Music Publishers Ltd
reprinted by permission

   (b) Add the time signature and missing bar-lines.

Schubert, *Seven Pieces in Fughetta Form*, No. 6

   (c) Add the time signature, and also the rests required to complete the bars at the places marked *.

Rubbra, Symphony No. 5

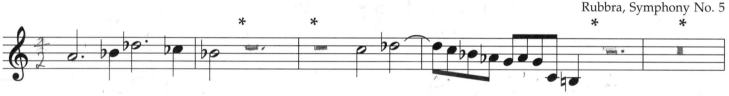

© 1949 Alfred Lengnick & Co. Ltd
reprinted by permission of Alfred Lengnick & Co. [a division of Complete Music Ltd]

2 **EITHER**

   (a) Write a rhythm on one note, with time signature and bar-lines, to fit these words.
        Write each syllable under the note or notes to which it is to be sung.

10

   Sweet and low, sweet and low,
   Wind of the western sea.   *Tennyson*

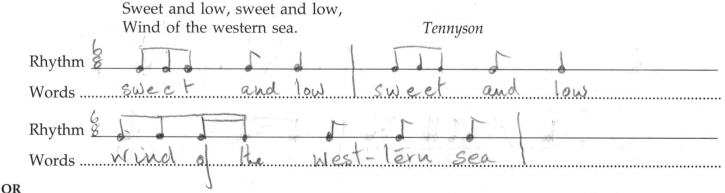

   OR

   (b) Write a four-bar rhythm in $\frac{6}{4}$ time. Include the following group of notes in your rhythm

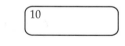 and also include a crotchet (quarter note) rest.

$\frac{6}{4}$

3 Name each of the following notes, as in the given example.

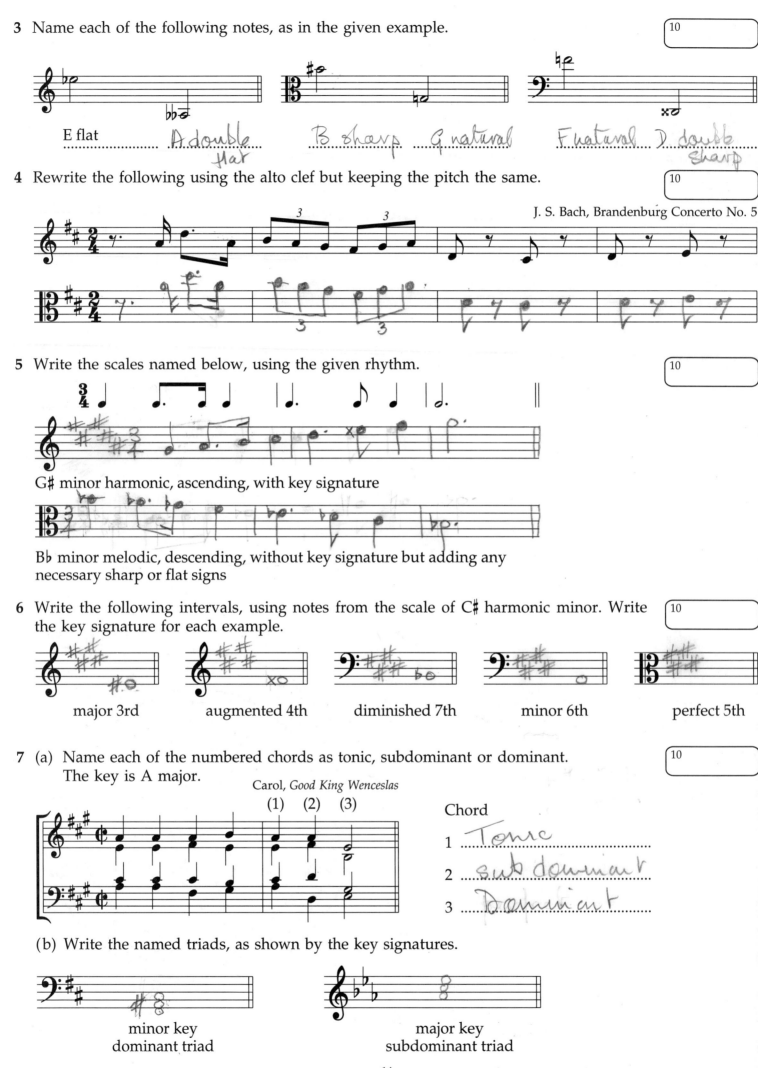

E flat .... A double Flat .... B sharp ...... G natural ...... F natural ...... D double Sharp ....

4 Rewrite the following using the alto clef but keeping the pitch the same.

J. S. Bach, Brandenburg Concerto No. 5

5 Write the scales named below, using the given rhythm.

G# minor harmonic, ascending, with key signature

Bb minor melodic, descending, without key signature but adding any necessary sharp or flat signs

6 Write the following intervals, using notes from the scale of C# harmonic minor. Write the key signature for each example.

major 3rd   augmented 4th   diminished 7th   minor 6th   perfect 5th

7 (a) Name each of the numbered chords as tonic, subdominant or dominant.
The key is A major.

Carol, *Good King Wenceslas*
(1)   (2)   (3)

Chord

1 ...... Tonic ....

2 ...... sub dominant ......

3 ...... Dominant ....

(b) Write the named triads, as shown by the key signatures.

minor key
dominant triad

major key
subdominant triad

14

8 This melody is taken from a movement called 'De l'aube à midi sur la mer' ('From dawn to noon on the sea') from Debussy's orchestral work *La Mer*. Look at it and then answer the questions below.

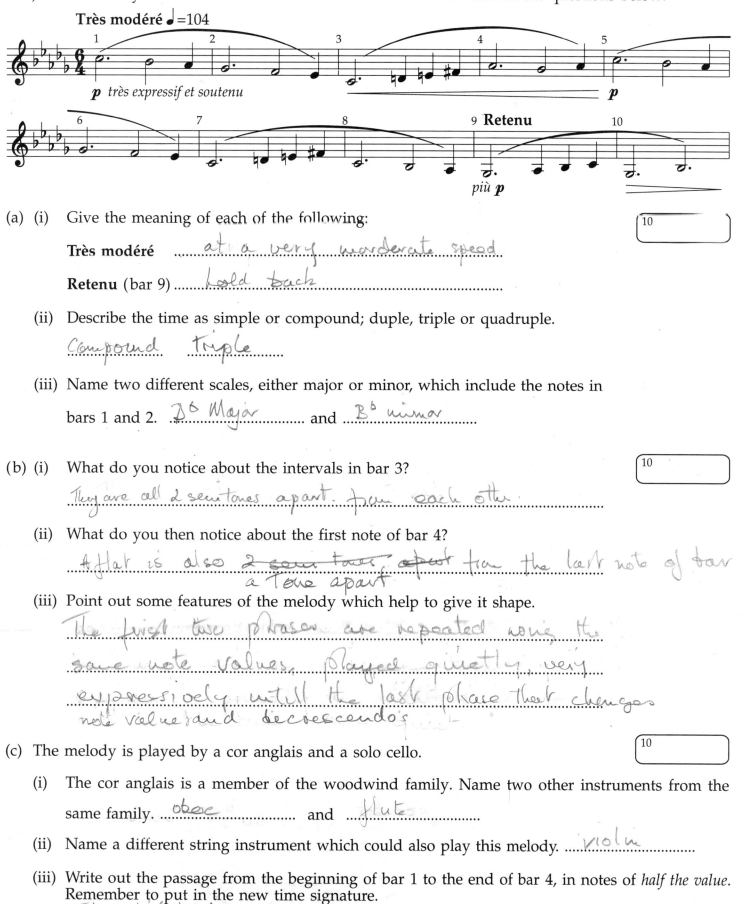

(a) (i) Give the meaning of each of the following:

   Très modéré ..... *at a very moderate speed* ..... [10]

   Retenu (bar 9) ..... *hold back* .....

(ii) Describe the time as simple or compound; duple, triple or quadruple.

   Compound   Triple

(iii) Name two different scales, either major or minor, which include the notes in

   bars 1 and 2. ..... *Db Major* ..... and ..... *Bb minor* .....

(b) (i) What do you notice about the intervals in bar 3? [10]

   They are all 2 semitones apart from each other.

(ii) What do you then notice about the first note of bar 4?

   A flat is also 2 semitones ~~apart~~ from the last note of bar
   a tone apart

(iii) Point out some features of the melody which help to give it shape.

   The first two phrases are repeated using the
   same note values, played quietly, very
   expressively until the last phrase that changes
   note values and decrescendo's

(c) The melody is played by a cor anglais and a solo cello. [10]

   (i) The cor anglais is a member of the woodwind family. Name two other instruments from the

   same family. ..... *oboe* ..... and ..... *flute* .....

   (ii) Name a different string instrument which could also play this melody. ..... *violin* .....

   (iii) Write out the passage from the beginning of bar 1 to the end of bar 4, in notes of *half the value*.
   Remember to put in the new time signature.

Printed in England by Headley Brothers Ltd,
The Invicta Press, Ashford, Kent and London

ISBN 1-85472-882-2

ABRSM PUBLISHING

**The Associated Board of
the Royal Schools of Music
(Publishing) Limited**

14 Bedford Square
London WC1B 3JG
United Kingdom